TECHNOLOGY, GADGETS AND INVENTIONS THAT YOU CAN MAKE

EXPERIMENTS BOOK FOR TEENS CHILDREN'S SCIENCE EXPERIMENT BOOKS

In this book, we're going to talk about some gadgets and inventions that you can make. So, let's get right to it!

Do you want to be an inventor when you grow up? There are plenty of inventions that you can make on your own with some simple supplies. Here are some ideas to get you started. Make sure you have an adult supervising whenever you do experiments or build inventions.

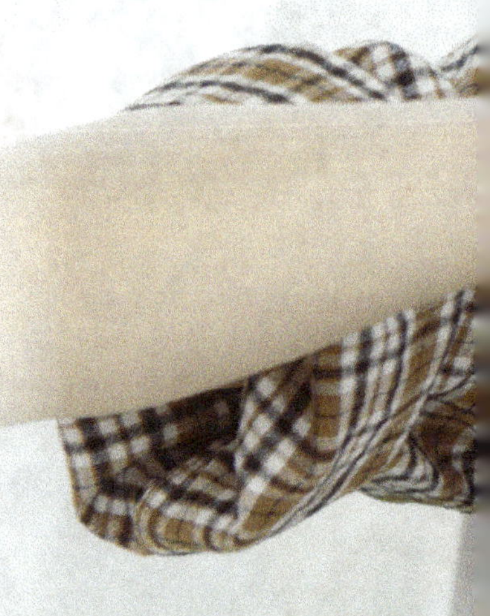

LED LIGHT

MAKE A BATTERY FROM SPARE PENNIES

In this experiment, you can make your own battery. Your battery will be powerful enough to power a small calculator or light up an LED light.

To make this battery, you'll need 14 pennies. The pennies need to be dated no earlier than 1982. That's because pennies before that date don't have enough zinc in them. You'll need some type of acidic liquid, such as lemon juice or vinegar. You'll need some cardboard, a pair of scissors, a screwdriver, and an inexpensive package of zinc washers about the same size as your pennies. You'll also need electrical tape, some aluminum foil, a simple calculator that you don't mind tearing apart, and an LED bulb.

PENNIES

WHAT TO DO

Step 1: Using your screwdriver, take the screws off the back of the calculator so that you can access the battery inside it.

Step 2: Take the battery out and set it aside. You can put it back after you test your new penny-powered battery.

Step 3: Pull the leads out of the calculator's casing. There will be a positive as well as a negative lead.

Step 4: Attach a wire to each lead. You can twist the wire around the end of the lead or use electrical tape to keep them together.

Step 5: Select four of the pennies and four of the washers. Trim out four pieces of cardboard into circular pieces just a little larger than the pennies.

Step 6: Soak the circular cardboard cutouts for a few minutes either in vinegar or lemon juice.

CUT CARDBOARD

Step 7: On your work surface, place a piece of aluminum foil. Then, stack one zinc washer on the top of it. Next, take one of the vinegar-soaked cardboard pieces and blot the excess liquid off, before placing it on top of the washer. Now, place your penny on the top of the cardboard.

You've created a small battery cell. The penny is positive and the zinc washer is negative with an electrolyte, the acid-soaked cardboard in between. You've used a similar process to the one used by Alessandro Volta when he invented the first battery in 1799.

ALESSANDRO VOLTA

Step 9: You can add cells by constructing another zinc-cardboard-penny stack on top of the one you just did. To power the small calculator, you'll probably need at least 4 cells.

Step 10: Each cell emits about 6/10 of a volt, so if you use 4 cells you'll have about 2.4 volts, which should be enough to power your calculator.

Step 11: Add wires to the top and bottom and use the electrical tape to keep your battery stack together. You can discard the piece of aluminum foil.

Step 12: Now it's time to connect your leads to the appropriate positive and negative leads on your calculator. If you've created your battery correctly, the calculator should power up! Test out a few addition and subtraction problems to see if your calculator is functioning properly.

Step 13: If your battery stops working, pull it apart and try soaking the pieces of cardboard in a little more vinegar.

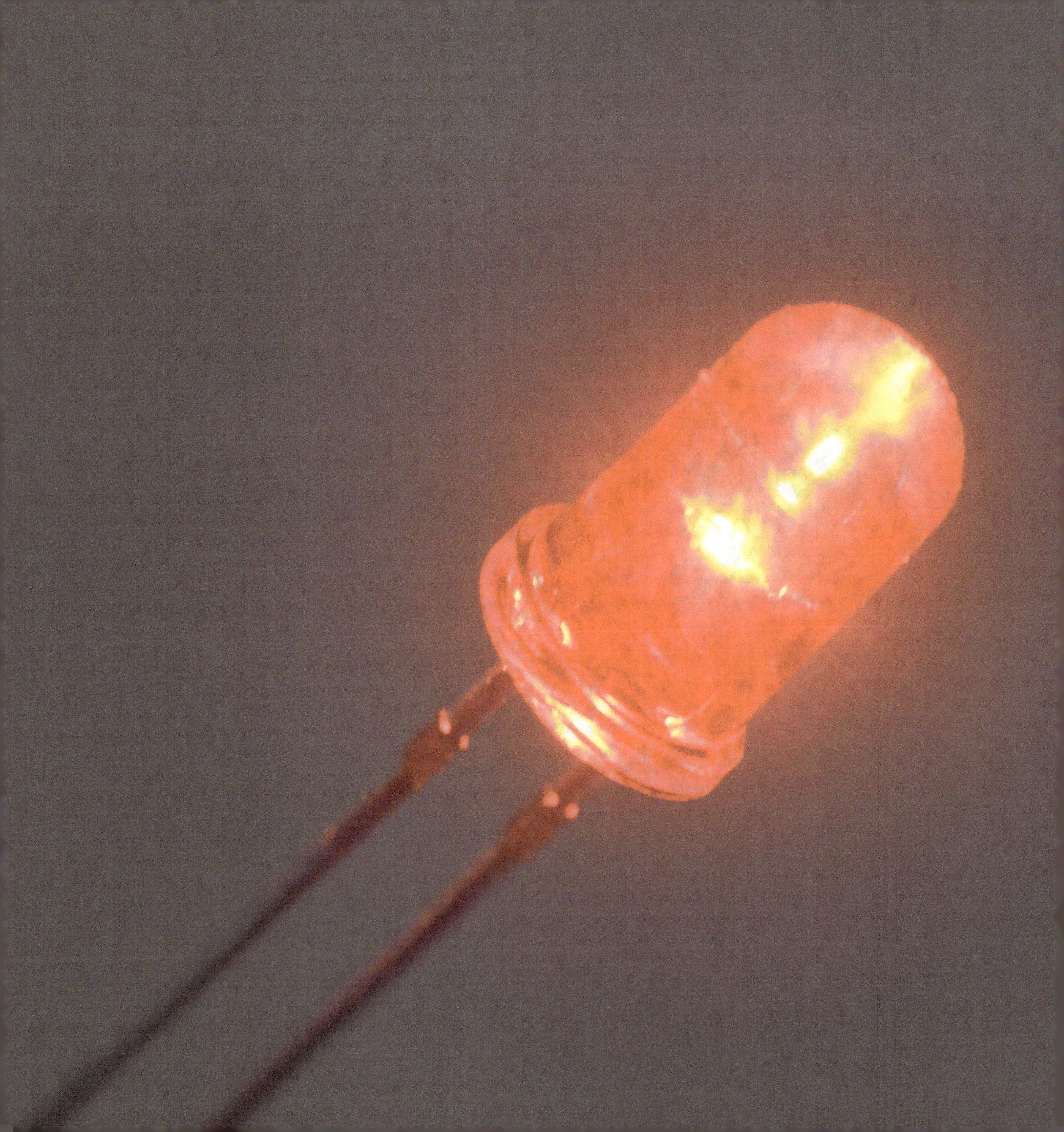

Step 14: Next, follow the same process to create a battery that has 14 cells. This battery should give you 14 x 0.6 volts or about 8.4 volts of power. This should be enough to light up your LED bulb. Place the taller leg of the LED to the top and the shorter to the bottom. Wrap your battery and bulb in electrical tape and see how long the LED stays lit. Some of them have stayed lit for more than a day!

BUILD A BIKE LIGHT THAT WORKS USING SOLAR POWER.

For this experiment, you'll use an empty deodorant container to make a light for your bike.

EMPTY DEODORANT CONTAINERS

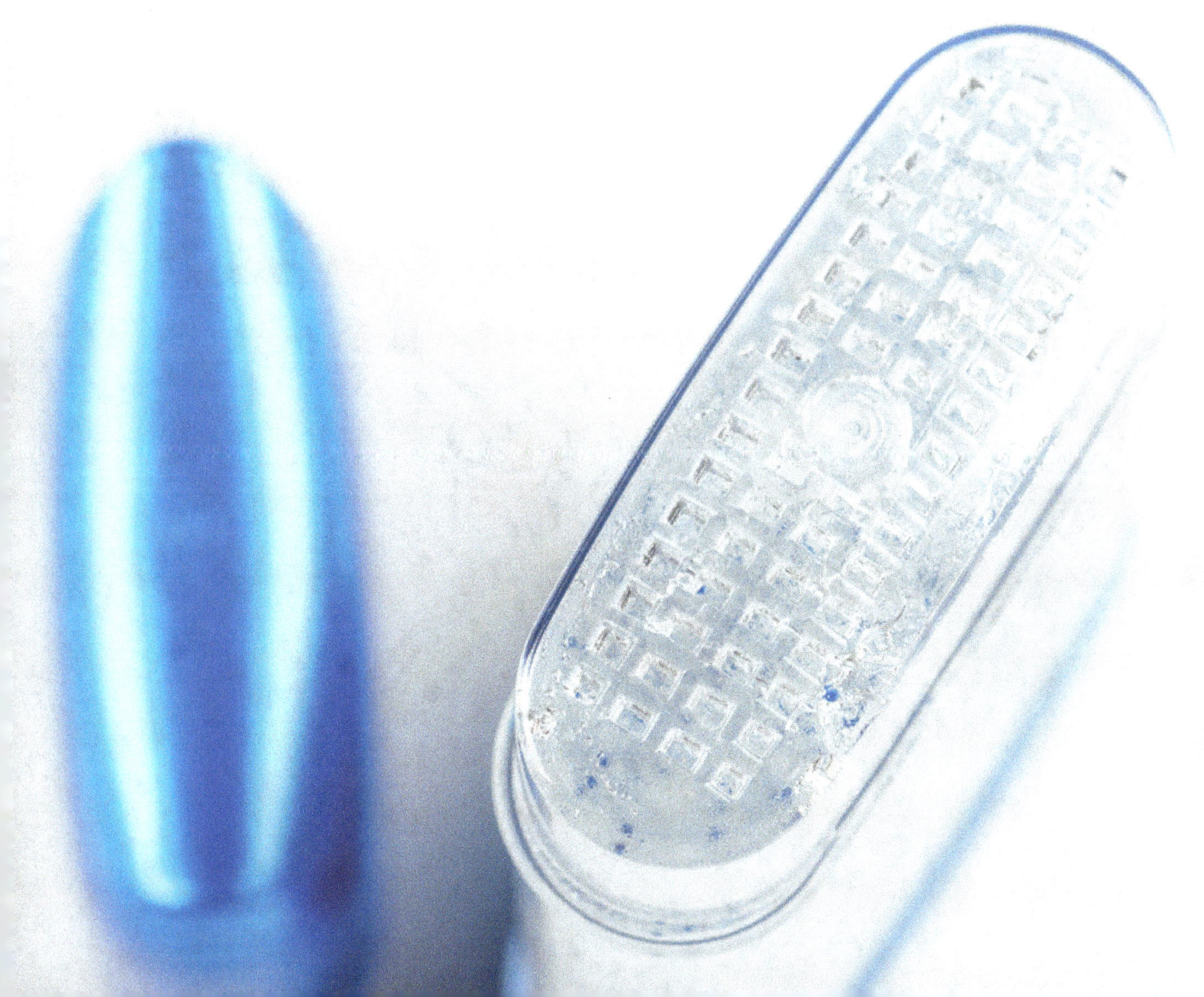

CLAMP
ELECTRIC SCREW DRIVER
SCREW DRIVER AND PLIER

What You'll Need

You'll need an empty deodorant container and a simple garden light that's powered by solar energy. You'll also need some silicone adhesive as well as an electric rotary tool that can cut plastic. Some hot glue is needed to hold the pieces in position. A screwdriver and a clamp are handy if you want to permanently clamp the light onto your bike.

WHAT TO DO

Step 1: Get rid of any leftover deodorant pieces that are in the container.

Step 2: Take out the plastic piece of the deodorant container that pushed the deodorant up to your armpit. There's a piece that holds the deodorant in place and a threaded spindle that pushes it up as the deodorant gets used *(see photo on the right page)*. If you do this properly, the inside of your deodorant container should be empty. Keep the deodorant cap. You're basically creating an area for the solar cell to reside.

SOLAR CELL

Step 3: Take your solar light apart. You should see a solar cell. The cell is attached to a circuit board. There should also be a battery pack.

Step 4: There's a small cell near the solar panel piece that is a light sensor. This cell acts like a switch. When it's dark outdoors, the light comes on. When it's sunny out, the light goes off and the battery gets charged from the sunlight.

PHOTOVOLTAIC SOLAR CELL

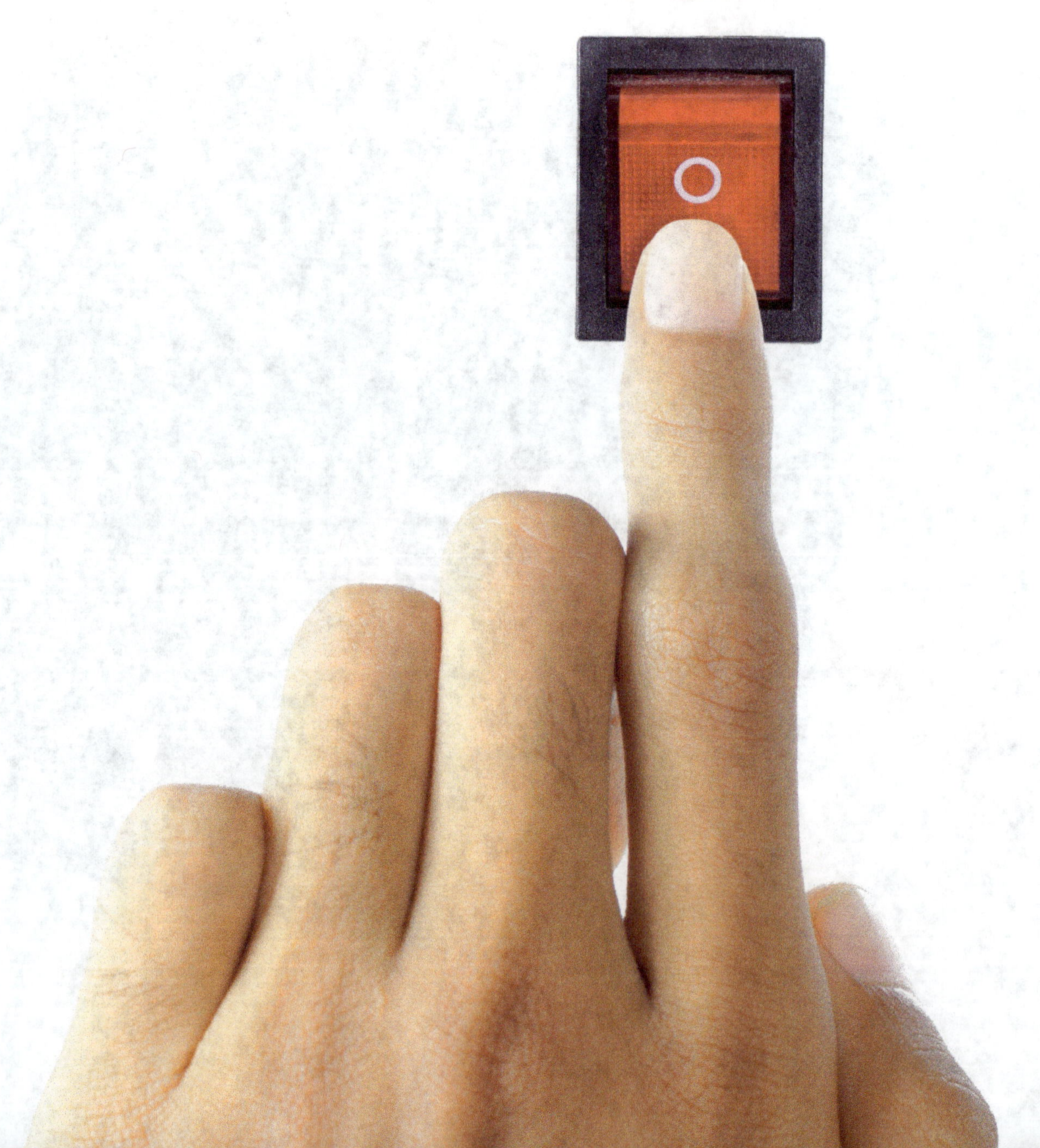

SWITCH

If you're really ambitious, you can wire a switch to this light sensor. Then, you could use the threaded spindle to turn the light sensor on or off. This way you could manually turn on the light when you want to ride your bike in conditions when it's partially dark out.

Step 5: Next, cut a hole in the back of the deodorant case where the ingredients are listed using a rotary tool designed to cut plastic. Make sure an adult is helping with this. You want the solar panel to fit tightly in the hole so it will face out of the body of the plastic deodorant case.

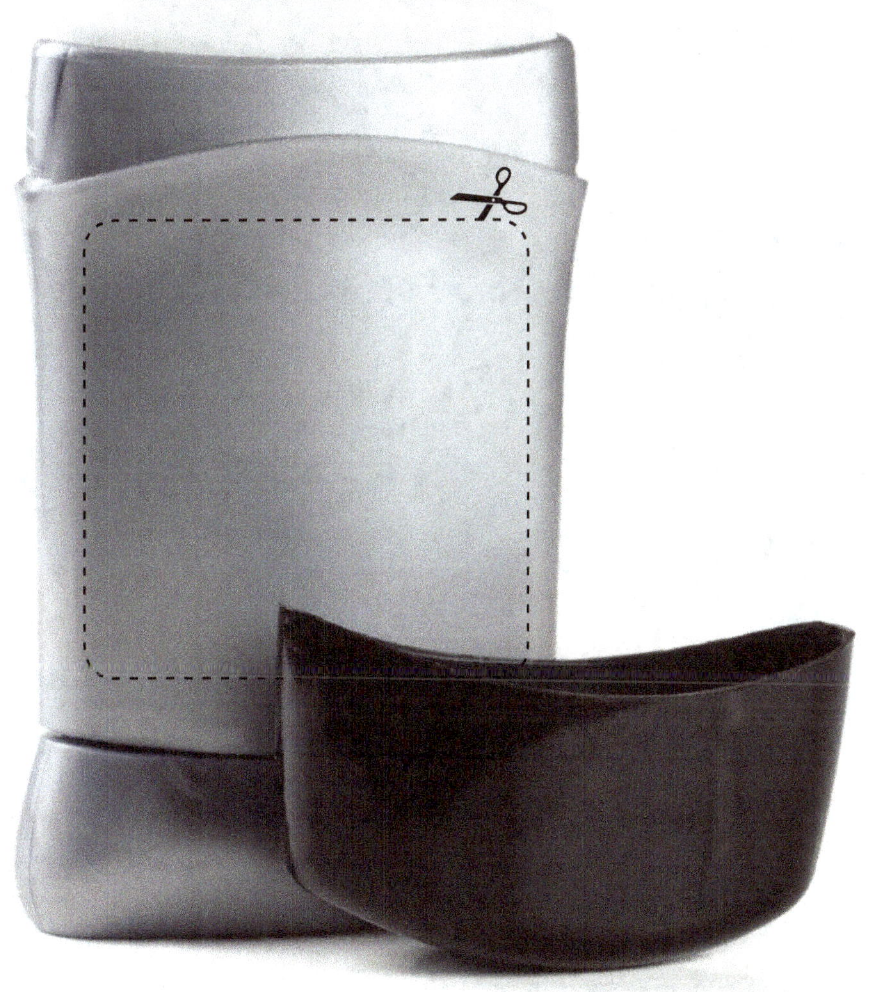

Step 6: The circuit board as well as the battery pack should fit inside the body of the plastic deodorant case. You can use hot glue to make the pieces stay in position until you have it all put together. The LED lights should be positioned where the deodorant used to be.

Step 7: Using some silicon adhesive, seal around the edges where the solar cell fits into the plastic case. The point of doing this is so water won't get in when you're riding your bike in the rain.

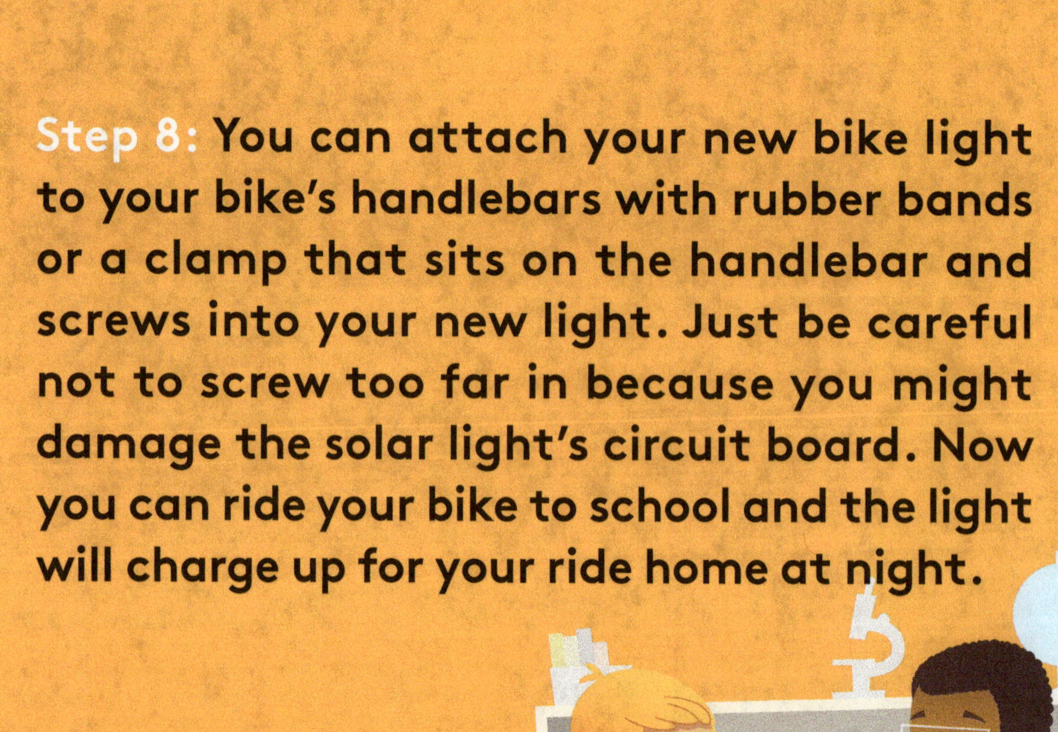

Step 8: You can attach your new bike light to your bike's handlebars with rubber bands or a clamp that sits on the handlebar and screws into your new light. Just be careful not to screw too far in because you might damage the solar light's circuit board. Now you can ride your bike to school and the light will charge up for your ride home at night.

LIGHT ATTACHED TO THE HANDLEBAR

METAL PERISCOPE

BUILD YOUR OWN PERISCOPE.

WHAT YOU'LL NEED

You'll need two mirrors. The size of the mirrors should be 2 inches by 1 inch but other sizes can also work. You'll need a carton or piece of cardboard that's about 6.5 inches wide and 8 inches in length.

You'll also need some scissors, strong glue, and some different colors of paint in green and brown to do a camouflage design when you're finished with the assembly.

Here's a template to help you as you do the assembly.

PERISCOPE

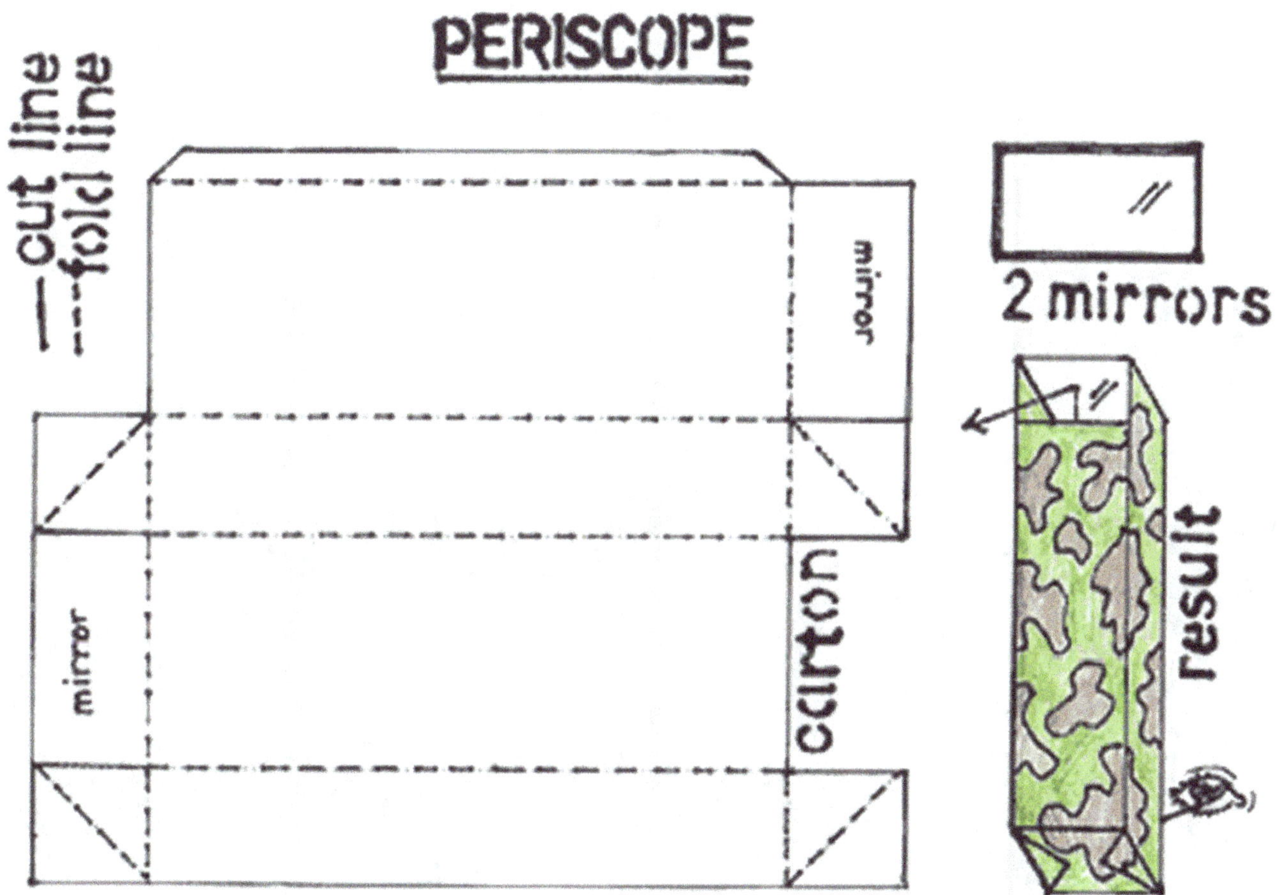

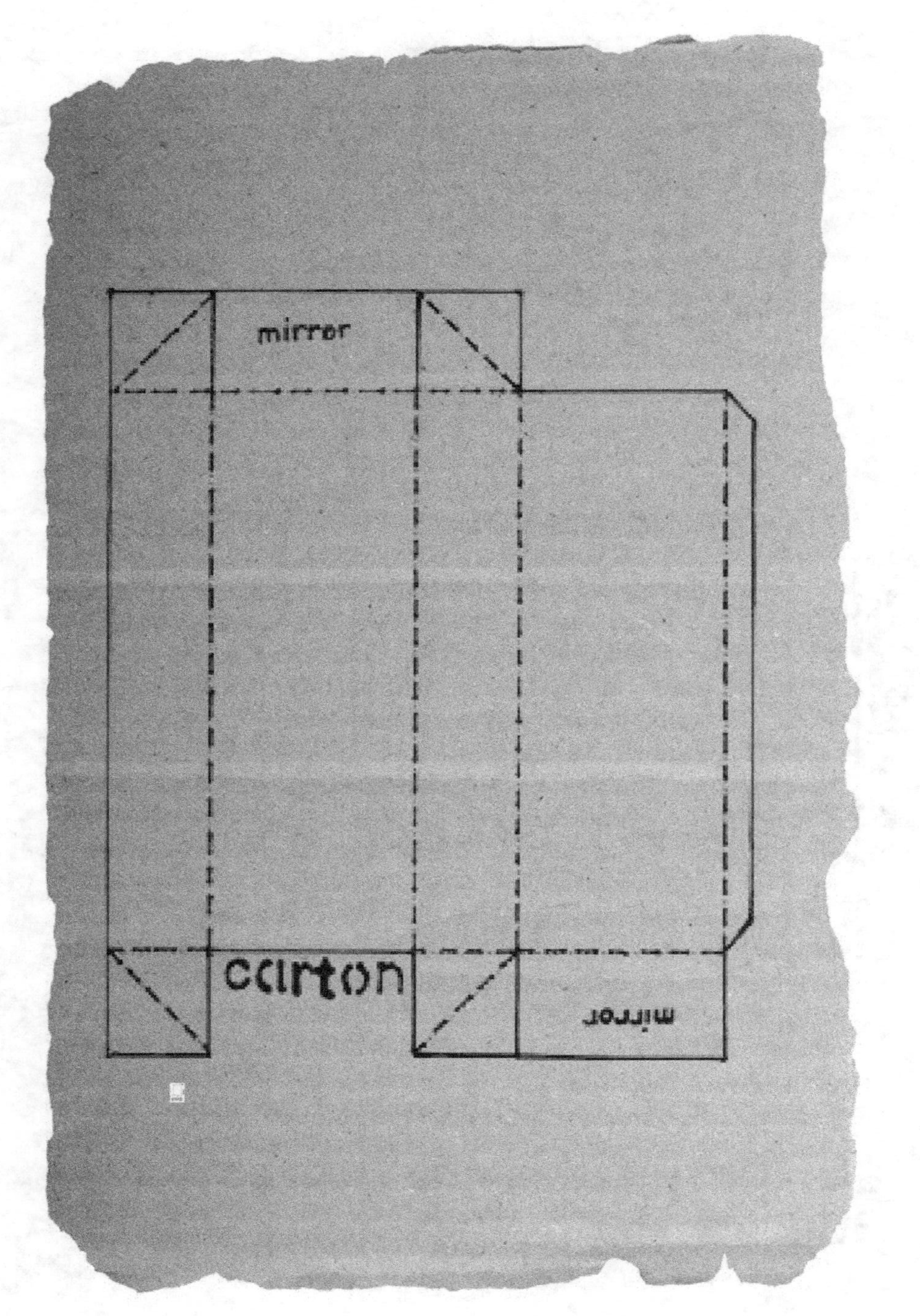

mirror
carton
mirror

WHAT TO DO

Step 1: Use the template to draw out your plan for the periscope on the carton or cardboard. The dashed lines mean you should fold along those lines and the lines that aren't dashed are lines that you'll need to cut.

Step 2: Once you have everything drawn out, place the mirrors in the right locations according to the template and then glue them down.

Step 3: Now, fold along the fold lines so that your flat piece becomes a box. If you've done it properly, one mirror should be facing up and the other should be facing down. Use glue to secure the edges so that your carton or cardboard stays box-shaped.

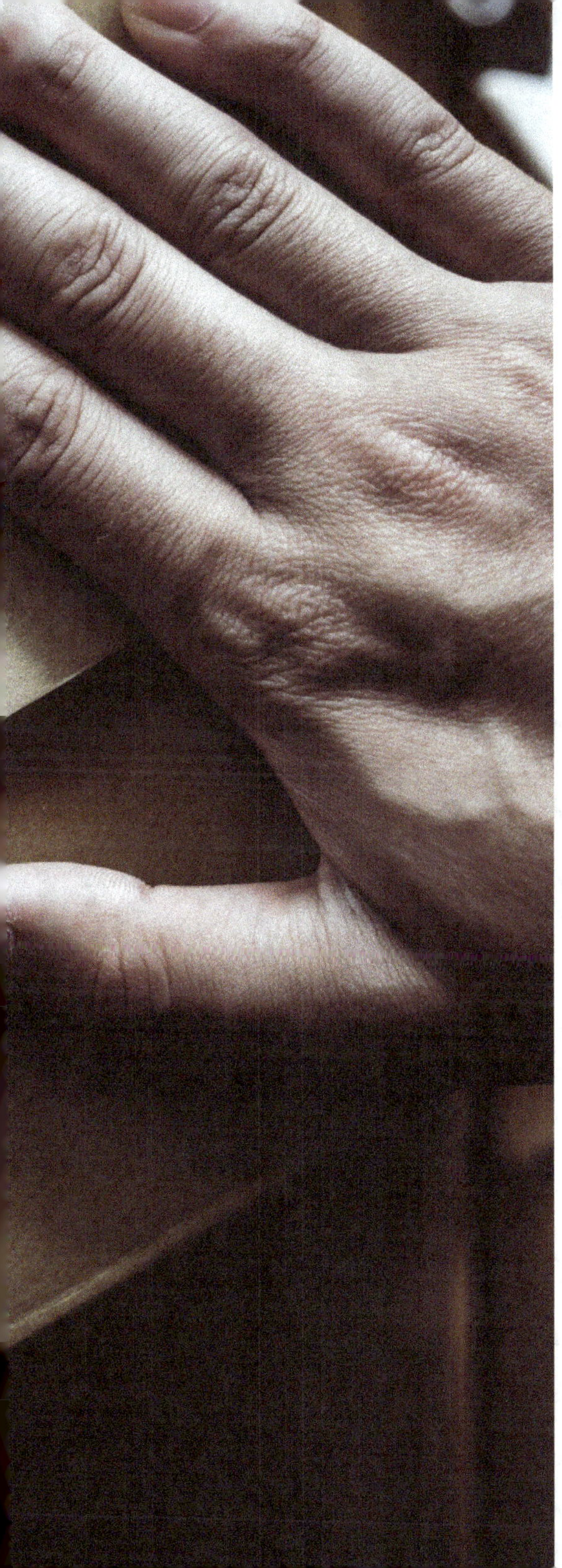

Fold each mirror so it's at a 45-degree angle. The mirrors should be parallel to each other. Fold in the side flaps and glue them so the mirrors will stay in position at 45-degree angles and parallel to each other.

PERISCOPE BOX

Step 5: Now, if you've assembled it correctly, your periscope should work. You can use it to see over a wall or a corner.

Step 6: Use paint to create a camouflage design for the outside of your periscope.

SUMMARY

If you think like an inventor, you'll notice there are lots of everyday items that with a little ingenuity can make interesting gadgets. These experiments will give you a starting point. Just make sure an adult supervises, especially when you use electrically powered cutting tools.

120°   140°   160°   180°   200°
20   30   10   20   30   10   20   30   10   20   30

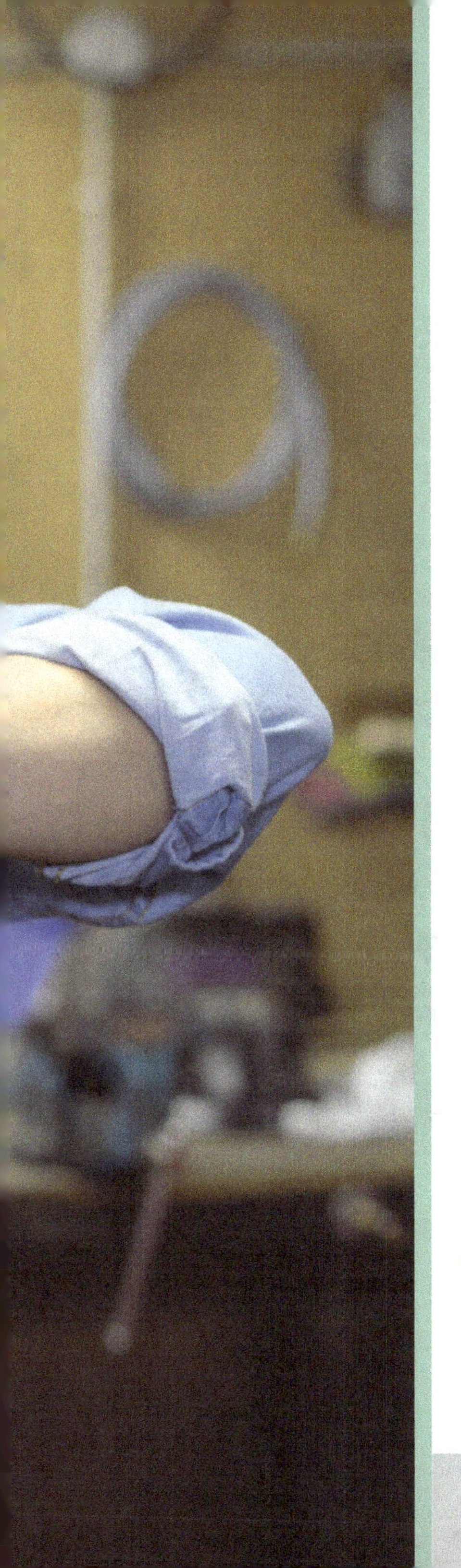

Awesome! Now that you've read about some inventions you can make, you may want to read about some new inventions on the market in the Baby Professor book, Pocket-Sized Technology - Gadgets That Fit

Visit

BABY PROFESSOR
EDUCATION KIDS

www.BabyProfessorBooks.com

to download Free Baby Professor eBooks
and view our catalog of new and exciting
Children's Books